DISCOVER ART
Pastels

DISCOVER ART
Pastels

Mike Chaplin
with Diana Vowles

Capella

Thanks to Gaynor Lloyd for the life drawings on pp. 34 and 44.

This edition published in 2007 by Arcturus Publishing Limited
26/27 Bickels Yard, 151–153 Bermondsey Street,
London SE1 3HA

Cover photography by Thomas Mitchell

ISBN: 978-1-84193-567-6

Printed in China

CONTENTS

INTRODUCTION

From the earliest times, the urge to make marks and leave a note to posterity led human beings to create art, and the natural earth pigments they used are still on the shelves in art shops in the 21st century. Early cave paintings were made by a technique that we see in the use of pastels today – in other words, pigment at its simplest being applied to a surface.

The Neolithic artists would often mix pigment with spittle in their mouths and then blow through their fingers to leave a negative shape of their hand on the wall; the spittle acting as a permanent glue as do the binders in modern pigments. Their remarkable paintings must have been done by the flickering light of some sort of candle, and their raw, vivid colours were no doubt necessary for the artists to be able to see their work as they painted it.

Centuries on, as paints were developed and art was restricted to religious subjects, pastel fell from favour; devotional and iconic art was done with no reference to a moving human form, and the artists could spend as long as they wished on its composition and finish. However, with the coming of humanism in the 14th century, the church finally allowed artists to make realistic depictions of people in movement. To do this they needed a technique that was direct, immediate and fast, and chalk in its various forms answered their needs. From that time on, it has remained the medium that many artists reach for when they want to make drawings that express spontaneity and movement, with the added benefit of a huge range of strong colour. It was a particular favourite of the Impressionist artist Edgar Degas (1834–1917), a brilliant draughtsman who used it for his many studies of ballet dancers, for which it was uniquely suited.

WORKING WITH PASTELS

Pastel is exciting and raw, harking back thousands of years to our basic instincts, but it is difficult. Although the techniques of applying it are very simple and direct, its intense, strong colours need careful handling. It is not possible to mix them together like paint, since the grains of the pigment will always remain separate, nor can you thin the colours down to make lighter tones. You can only make a pastel lighter or darker than it inherently is by scumbling one colour on top of another to make a mix that will be seen by the eye as a single colour. So, unlike watercolour painting, where you can buy two or

My copy of one of the paintings in the caves at Lascaux in southern France shows that the Neolithic artists were capable of sophisticated life drawings, full of energy and power.

three tubes of pigment and mix them together easily to make different colours and thinning them with water to vary the tone, when you are working with pastel you will be faced with making early decisions about what pigments, and tones of those pigments, you will need.

Consequently, pastel can seem daunting for the beginner, and the aim of this book is to guide you through the early steps of mastering its use. It is a wonderfully direct and expressive medium that encourages you to work large and bold, and as such you may find that it transforms your work in other media too.

The book includes not just dry pastels but also charcoal, watercolour pencils and pastels and oil pastels. It leads you to explore a range of techniques from basic mark-making, to using warm and cool colours to express emotion and give your pictures an appearance of three dimensions; you will discover the fascination of organic shapes and of man-made industrial forms. Most of all, you will enjoy the qualities of pastel that have led artists to employ it over many centuries.

This detail drawn from *Ballerina and Lady with a Fan* (1885) by Edgar Degas demonstrates pastel's capability for catching spontaneity and movement, together with vibrant colour.

DRAWING TOOLS

Manufacturers offer pastels in about 200 colours and, since it is not possible for the artist to reduce the tone as is done with paint, each of the colours is available in five different tones from light to dark. In practice you will probably find three adequate, but this still leaves the beginner with a bewildering choice. Fortunately, useful starter sets are available, some of them including a brush, an eraser, some paper and a pencil sharpener. Starter sets are usually designed for a particular purpose, such as one for figures which has a range of flesh tones or a landscape selection with a choice of greens.

To make pastels, the pigment is mixed with binder in a vat. It is then extruded like spaghetti and chopped into short lumps or compressed into moulds, which produce much harder pastels. The latter are best for tight drawing with hard edges, while the soft ones are ideal for scumbling rich areas of colour. Hardest of all are pastel pencils, which have a wood casing.

Watercolour pastels and pencils are in effect watercolour paints, while oil pastels are compressed oil colour. They are a means of applying paint conveniently put into a drawing medium.

CHARCOAL

Charcoal is available in various grades, from hard to soft, and in thin wands or thick stumps. It is usually made from willow, but you can even draw with barbecue charcoal if it has not been treated with lighter fuel. It is messy to use but produces wonderfully rich velvety blacks.

These three marks are made with Sap Green in tones 1, 3 and 4.

If you decide to buy individual colours I recommend these for a basic set, plus black and white. It includes a warm and cool version of each colour, and you will need a light and dark tone of every one.

1. Cadmium Red
2. Alizarin Crimson
3. Cadmium Yellow
4. Lemon Yellow
5. Sap Green
6. Hooker's Green
7. Cerulean Blue
8. Cobalt Blue
9. French Ultramarine
10. Burnt Carmine

The top zigzags are drawn with a compressed cake of hard pastel; the middle are soft pastel; the bottom are pastel pencil, which is the hardest of all. To the right of each, they have been rubbed out with a putty eraser. The zigzags have been smudged in three different ways, from left to right, with a soft dry brush, a finger and a stump.

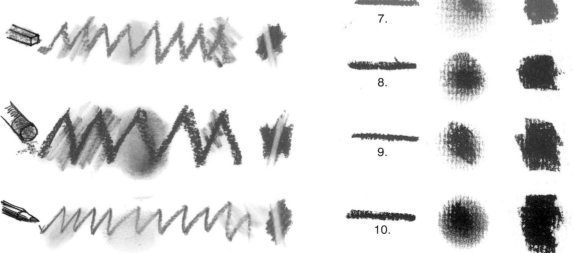

To adhere to the surface, dry pastels need a paper with a rough texture. You will be able to apply up to four coats before a smooth chalky surface builds up, making it difficult to put more pastel down. Some artists draw on very fine carborundum paper of the kind used on car bodywork, which is strong enough to be used with wet pastels. If you are working with dry pastels you can even draw on fine sandpaper. Be experimental, but also be aware that your work may not last as long as on art paper.

Because watercolour and oil pastels have gum and oil respectively in them they are quite sticky and can be used on smoother surfaces.

Artists drawing with pastel commonly work on mid-toned paper, when all their marks become positive statements about light and dark tones. Many papers are available, offering a range of tones and colours. You can buy spiral-bound blocks with the drawing paper interleaved with waxy paper to prevent the pastel transferring to the back of the facing sheet.

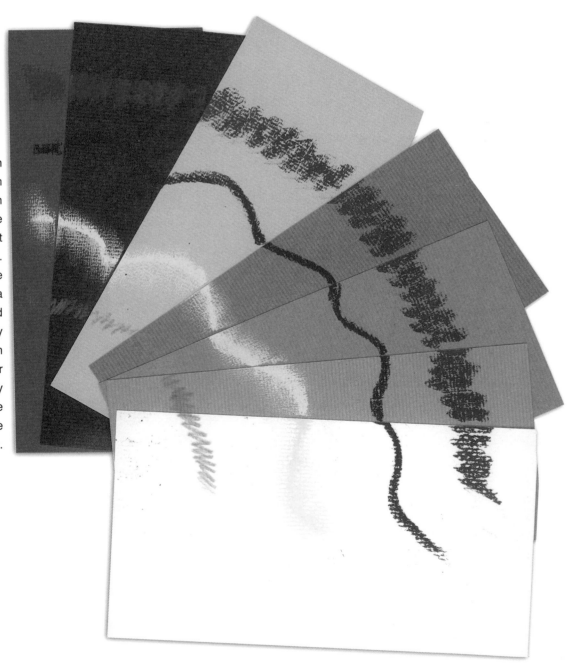

EQUIPMENT AND WORKSPACE

Pastel is a messy medium, and if you will be using it in your house rather than a studio you will need to put down a dustsheet to protect your carpet. Wear a mask if you are making vigorous drawings with dry pastel and never blow dust off your work. I keep a vacuum cleaner beside me and when dust builds up on the surface of the drawing I run the hose close to it to suck up the dust. You may find a mini vacuum cleaner of the type used for computers a useful investment.

You will need a board to rest your paper on, and the problem of dust will be lessened if you tilt it upwards. If you are on a limited budget you can make do with a couple of bricks on a table, but buying a proper easel will allow you to angle your board a few degrees forward from the vertical, which will be a great help.

BLENDERS

You can blend pastels with your finger, cotton buds, a blending stump or a brush. Stumps, or torchons, are available in art shops, but you can make your own by rolling a strip of paper into a tight wad. A soft fan or blending brush is excellent for brushing soft powder across the paper to the exact spot you want it to be.

FIXATIVE

Fixatives are available in aerosols and in liquid form, for which you will need a diffuser. This is made of two tubes hinged at right angles. One tube goes in the fixative and you blow through the other, creating a vacuum which draws the fixative upwards to be dispersed in a fine spray when it encounters the air flow.

When you are fixing repeatedly and adding more coats of pastel you will clog up the paper if you apply too much fixative. Hold it 60 cm (2 ft) away and use just enough to stop the pastel falling off.

Fixative also allows you the creative use of dust. You can sandpaper a pastel stump above the paper to cover it with dust, then draw into it with a comb or other implement. You can even sprinkle dust down through paper doilies or stencils you have made yourself. You will obviously have to spray very gently to avoid spoiling your pattern.

If you are sketching on location with no fixative to hand, a can of hairspray will do the job. Don't use it for finished work as it may yellow or otherwise degrade the paper.

You can use an eraser as a drawing tool to put lights into darks but of course this must be done before you spray with fixative.

SHARPENERS

You will need a knife for sharpening stumps, and it will also be useful for scratching out pastel to reveal the paper or colour beneath. You can buy pencil sharpeners large enough for pastels, but hard, brittle pastel flakes when you try to sharpen it and using sandpaper is the best option here.

ORGANIZING YOUR WORKSPACE

It is best to have your own private workspace for any form of art so that you can leave your equipment and ongoing pictures out, ready for you to go straight to work even if you only have half an hour to spare. However, with pastels it is essential to keep them safely away from children and pets. A window giving north light is the ideal, since you will not be troubled by glare or by shadows moving across your paper. For drawing after dark, buy some daylight bulbs rather than using ordinary household bulbs, which have a pronounced yellow cast.

For keeping your paper clean and dry, a zipped folder from an art shop is practical and also spacesaving, since you can store it upright. A locked cupboard to keep knives, pastels and fixative safely stored is advisable if there are children in the house.

When you stand up for long drawing sessions, spread your feet so that your weight is evenly distributed. If you are right-handed, look past the left side of your board at your subject and vice versa. The artist here has his board leaning forward to shed dust, but it is set too low – try to have your eye in the centre of the paper.

BASIC MARKS

LINEAR MARKS

In the sampler of marks below I have worked light on dark. If you have previously drawn only dark marks on white paper you will probably find this quite an alien way of thinking. However, it is a technique that is much used when working with pastel, so try practising these easy marks on midtoned paper to accustom yourself to it.

Hatching (a series of parallel lines to add tone).

Scumbling (working the pastel in circles).

Sharp, jabbing strokes.

Cross-hatching, to deepen tone made by hatching.

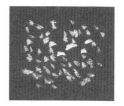

Pivoting a short piece of pastel on the paper.

Sharp, jabbing marks.

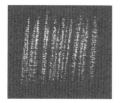

Simple strokes with the point of a hard, sharp pastel.

Pastel smudged with a finger.

Marks made by rocking the flat end of a hard pastel.

Spots drawn with the end of a pastel.

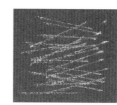

Lines made by striking with the side of the pastel.

A simple full stroke of the width of the pastel.

I drew the vertical lines with a pastel then zigzagged with a stump, picking up colour.

I made the square with the edge of a pastel, then pulled the lines out from it with a stump.

Using orange pastel I drew staccato lines, giving a busy effect. I then took a blue pastel and made long, sweeping movements. On the left, the eye can easily distinguish between the two lines. On the right, a third line has created a confusing jumble.

AREAS OF COLOUR

The marks below look simple, but they are very important because once you have done them successfully you will have covered all the basic ways of putting pastel down.

However, as you gain confidence with the medium I hope you will want to try experimental mark-making in order to build up your own personal vocabulary.

A simple mark pulled from the side of a short piece of pastel.

Here the mark has been smudged with a finger.

Drawn with the side of the pastel, with harder pressure on the left.

Red has been added, with harder pressure exerted on the right.

Here the red and blue have been smudged together with a finger.

Using the same paper, I smudged with my finger but some of the paper is still showing through the colour.

This time I wetted the pastel so it flooded over the paper, leaving no grain showing.

This mark was made on rough paper so strong I could not press the pastel down.

In this picture of the Venice lagoon at sunset, the colour at the top of the sky has been rubbed in, whereas at the horizon the sky is slightly broken so the eye travels into it. Linear marks in the foreground pull the eye forward.

SKETCHBOOKS AND FORMAT

You will need sketchbooks for making notes, trying out your ideas and recording scenes you might want to make a finished drawing of later. Buy two, one square and one upright bound, to give you a wide choice of format, and try to find ones with a variety of paper in them. If you cannot, clip loose sheets of paper to your board instead. Because your sketches are for your eyes only, they are a chance to enjoy being spontaneous and experimental.

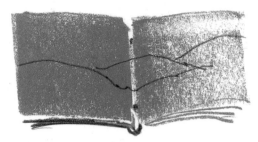

A square sketchbook offers you a square or panoramic format. With an upright bound sketchbook you can work within a square, a portrait oblong or a landscape oblong.

Pastel is a convenient way to carry colour, and here I have used it to make colour notes on a pen drawing. Do not feel you have to fit the paper manufacturer's format; I chose to end my sketch at the tree, giving me a format within which I often work.

After I had been watching horse racing one day I realized that the flowing shapes I was making in my sketchbook resembled horses' legs. This sketch isn't intended to be accurate but to express the energy and fluidity of horses.

This sketch of St Paul's Cathedral in London was done on the spot but in a more considered way than the swift impression of the horses shown above. I began by scrubbing in pure, strong, broad bands of colour to establish the emotional feel of the subject matter, adding the drawing afterwards.

COLOUR

The colours you use in your pastels will to some extent be governed by the scene you are portraying but will also reflect your personal choice. However, colours also convey a psychological message that will affect the viewer's emotional response to your work. Reds, oranges and browns are described as warm, being associated with heat and fire, while blues and greys are cool, recessive colours that allow you to give a sense of distance as well as mood.

The colour wheel contains the full spectrum of colours, as seen in a rainbow. Blue, red and yellow are primary colours and cannot be produced by mixing other colours. On the wheel they are separated by their secondary colours: red and blue make purple, blue and yellow make green, and red and yellow make orange. These are complementary to the primaries opposite them on the wheel.

Paint colours can be mixed in a palette, but with pastels you have to mix them on the paper instead. Always put the lighter colour down first as you cannot successfully pull a lighter colour over a darker one.

Green mixed by putting down yellow then pulling blue across the texture of the paper.

Green made from blue and yellow blended with a finger; the result lacks liveliness.

Seen from a distance, these dots of yellow and blue give a fresh, vibrant green.

Complementary colours: green and red.

Complementary colours: orange and blue.

Complementary colours: purple and yellow.

Mixing complementary colours produces greys, and here I used purple and yellow for some of the recessive greys in this sketch of the Louvre, made on grey cardboard.

I drew this sketch with dry pastel but spread the colour out with water to make the soft, warm areas against the quite hard-edged blue areas. Warm colours advance, so they are normally found in the foreground, with blues receding behind them. However, because the blue here is hard-edged, with tonally dark lines in it, it comes forward from the warmer colour, which is tonally flat. Both colours are overridden by the dark charcoal of the fountain in the foreground.

TONE

By tone, we mean how light or dark objects are, governed by the amount of light falling upon them. We can use tone to show the form of an object and to set the mood of a picture; extremes of tone are dramatic, while close tones give a gentle mood. Because we cannot alter the tone of pastels we have to buy each colour in a range of tones. Five are normally provided, though the set shown below has a sixth in the form of white.

| Ivory Black | French Grey (Full) | French Grey (Mid) | French Grey (Light) | French Grey (Pale) | Chinese White |

This bonfire scene relies on tone to present the main impact, and the colours have been considered as much for their tonal value as for their colour content. The dark shapes of the silhouetted figures emphasize the brilliance of the light from the bonfire, while the cold dark blue of the surrounding darkness contrasts with the hot red flames. I used a midtoned blue paper as a surface, against which the light colours of the fire showed up clearly and gained added drama.

| Sepia | Burnt Umber | Umber | Chocolate | Terracotta | Brown Ochre |

For this sketch I used a manufacturer's set of browns. The range of tones in the tree branches gives depth, creating layers of lines that the eye sees through. I created form in the tree trunks by drawing with different colours and tones. The tree was drawn dark on light, while in the grass below there are light marks on dark. These can be made by indenting the paper with a fingernail, a knitting needle or other point and then rubbing pastel flat on to the paper so that it does not dip into the lines.

DRY PASTELS AS A WET MEDIUM

Pastel is generally thought of as a drawing medium that is used dry. However, you can use it with water, crossing the boundary between drawing and painting.

Pastels can become quite hard over time, and if you try to use a set that has been stored for a while, be warned that you may find it more difficult to dissolve them in water.

After putting swatches of dry pastel down, I softened them with a brush dipped in clean water and pulled out pigment from each of the tones. I was able to achieve only limited distance and tonal range.

I dipped pastel in water to make a wet medium to draw with, rubbing until I had used all the available moist pastel. This method allowed me to spread and blend the colour over a much bigger area, with richer colour and texture.

Using rough paper, I put pink pastel down then worked watercolour over it, pulling the brush in different directions. The pastel dissolved to a soft pink glow.

After putting down pastel, I laid blue over the left-hand side in one stroke and dried it quickly with a hairdryer. The pastel has retained its characteristic marks.

I created this apple by putting down an orange wash of watercolour then working into it with green pastel while it was still wet.

Pastels sit very comfortably with watercolour, and many watercolourists carry them for making notes. This picture is a mixture of watercolour and pastel drawing, some put in while the paint was wet and some added afterwards. Because I was drawing loosely on rough watercolour paper few of the lines are hard, so the pastel blends well with the soft qualities that are associated with watercolour. In the foreground grasses there are light marks on dark, added to give this area a lift.

To create a sense of space in the foliage, I drew some soft lines in wet paint and added harder ones when it was dry.

I built up light textures on dark with fluid marks, varying the pressure to make hard and soft lines that give depth.

RESISTS AND TEXTURES

RESISTS

Sometimes we need to reserve areas in a picture where the pigment cannot reach the paper. This can be done by laying a physical resist such as a paper mask on the paper or by relying on the antipathy between two different media. For example, most graphite pencils have a slight oiliness to them, and if you make a drawing first with a 6B pencil and then pull the side of a dry pastel across it you will find that where the grain of the paper has been filled by the soft, greasy graphite the pastel has been unable to adhere to it.

Another way of creating a resist is to use masking fluid, primarily used by watercolourists. It is removed by rubbing, and it is quite easy to take it off by mistake when you rub pastel over it. To avoid this, sandpaper pastel over the drawing then use fixative or water to fix the pastel dust.

I drew this tree with 6B pencil then pulled the sides of blue and yellow pastels across it. The linear work with the pencil has remained intact, with the pastel creating a haze of colour around it.

These white shapes were created by cutting shapes in low-tack tape with a scalpel. I lifted them off after rubbing over the area with pastel and fixing it.

TEXTURES

Pastel used on rough paper will give you exciting textures, but you can capitalize on this further by using watercolour texture paste, available from art shops in tubes or jars. It is a white or clear paste which you can spread on the paper with a spatula and work into while it is wet. Experiment with various textures, perhaps disturbing it with a stick or corrugated paper or pressing fabric such as muslin into it. When it hardens, leaving a raised texture which prevents the pigment reaching the surface of the paper, rub dry pastel into it with your finger.

I used a mixture of watercolour and pastel in this sketch of a building with shuttered windows. I used texture paste to give the feeling of rough masonry, rubbing dry powdered pastel into it with my finger when it had hardened.

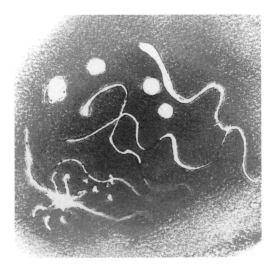

Masking fluid creates hard-edged whites and because of the accuracy with which you can apply it, using an old brush, it is useful for reserving fine lines.

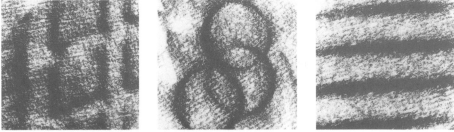

Making rubbings by laying paper over various items and rubbing pastel on top will make you aware of textures. Even something as mundane as a car tyre will help to train your eye.

ORGANIC SHAPES

Nature presents us with a much bigger choice of visual experiences than we could ever invent, and by going outdoors to work you will find many shapes and colours that are worth investigation. I structure my working time to allow me time to learn, which is a never-ending process for an artist. Setting daily tasks as I do such as making a linear study, a colour study, a tonal study, an exterior scene and so forth will give a point to the work you do that day and help to focus your mind on what you are trying to achieve in every sketch. Allow yourself plenty of variety by choosing different subjects or techniques each day.

I took a photograph of this scene because I liked the contrast of the hard vertical reeds with the soft horizontals of the water ripples. The goose provided a touch of narrative.

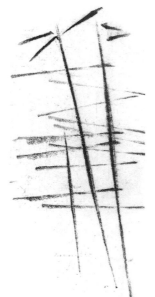

I continued to build up tone in the water and added variation to the angles of the reeds. The goose is a very simple shape with a tall neck and an indication of a small head. Curving lines in the water in front of it show that it is in motion.

The photograph makes the subject matter look complicated, but tackled as a flat linear pattern it is easily transcribed into soft horizontal marks drawn softly and slowly and darker vertical marks put in with jabbing strokes.

FLOWERS

You can find a huge variety of texture, colour and form in floral subjects, from the fresh crispness of a bluebell to the sagging, browning petals of an overblown rose. For an artist, decaying plant matter is just as worthy of study as the most perfect bloom.

The extremes of tone make this a dramatic study of a lily that almost verges on the abstract. Working with a close tonal range would have evoked a very different, softer feel.

CHANGING SCALE

For small, intimate studies done indoors, keep a box of objects that appeal to you. Collect them for specific aesthetic reasons – for example, shells chosen for their colour, shape or repetitive linework. Art can happen on a tabletop, so there is no need to look for grand subjects.

Out of doors, you will find many of the same textures and rhythms within the landscape. Working on a larger scale will give you the chance for strong, gestural marks.

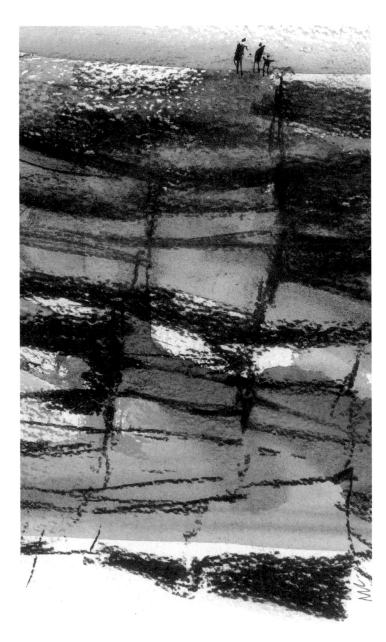

Because this drawing of three shells at various stages of completion is an objective study of colour, I needed to be very precise about the pigments I chose in order to achieve accuracy.

Umber

Burnt Carmine

Terracotta Dark

Terracotta Light

French Grey

Spectrum Blue

I felt the abstract qualities of stratified rocks were best expressed by using charcoal on rough paper to give a strong, dynamic piece. I put down pastel over the charcoal, dissolving it in places to vary the texture. The same strata would be found in even a small piece of rock from the same landscape, and without the simple figures at the top of the cliff the viewer would have no indication as to scale.

MAN-MADE SHAPES

While most people would regard man-made objects such as cranes, cooling towers and pylons as blots on the landscape, for the artist they present the opportunity to manipulate large areas of strong colour or tone and balance them against the elegance of linear rhythms. If you study industrial scenes with an eye to making a composition from them, you will be surprised by how aesthetically interesting they often are.

These power station cooling towers, seen across a wide river, made strong, dramatic shapes. I drew them with pencil and quickly applied pastel. Placing the towers at the top meant that the bulk of the composition is about the largely empty space of the water, with the reflection of the towers supplying interest in the middle distance. Done across both pages of my sketchbook, this large study is full of interest in texture, colour, line and tone.

The dramatic linear quality of the pylons is enhanced by the dark bulk of the bushes and the darkening sky behind.

The electricity cables running across the top of the picture push the tonal masses of the towers back into the distance.

I am intrigued by lines seen against the sky on building sites. The lozenges of browns and blues make an interesting design in themselves.

This detail from a painting of a container port shows the cranes that lift containers from lorries below, with little figures indicating their huge scale. After laying watercolour washes, I drew with pastel and charcoal to translate the vigour of the objects into the method of drawing them.

I often include pastels in my travelling kit, and when I came upon this scene of boats pulled up in a little creek I instinctively reached for them because I wanted the composition to be about full-strength tone, full-strength colour and plenty of linear interest. It is done entirely in pastel, some smudged and some hard-edged.

PERSPECTIVE

LINEAR PERSPECTIVE

A basic understanding of perspective will help you to give a three-dimensional feel to your pictures. The most important things to remember are that, rather than being a fixed point, the horizon line will always be on your eye level and that all objects will diminish in size as they recede from the foreground towards the horizon.

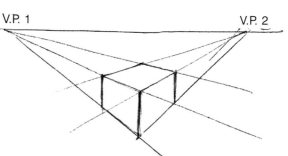

In single-point perspective, parallel lines converge towards the horizon and meet at the vanishing point.

When an object is side-on rather than parallel to you, two-point perspective comes into play. Lines extended from the sides of the object converge at two vanishing points.

This sketch of the opera house in Paris is a loose study in single-point perspective. The little linear figure to the left of the lamp post represents my position if I were to walk directly forwards from my sketching point.

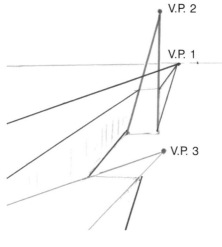

In this drawing the lines of the flat surfaces obey the rules of single-point perspective. If a plane is rising in front of you the vanishing point will be above the horizon; if it is going down away from you the vanishing point will be below it.

AERIAL PERSPECTIVE

Atmospheric conditions make objects lose their strength of tone and colour as they recede from us until eventually they are little more than pale, hazy outlines. Edges and details soften and colours become cooler. Remember that aerial perspective also affects the sky; overhead, it is dark blue, becoming lighter towards the horizon.

Dark tones in the foreground recede through mid to light tones in the distance. When colour is introduced, the perspective is reinforced by the progression from warm colours in the foreground to cool blues and greys in the far distance.

My sketch of a Tuscan landscape demonstrates the use of aerial perspective in a composition. The strong tones, warm colours and defined details are in the foreground, while the distance is little more than diffused cool blues.

SIMPLE LANDSCAPES

The two landscapes shown here are quite similar in that they are both concerned with the seaside and people at leisure in that setting. However, they have very different horizon lines and the view of the cliffs is therefore from different angles. When you are making a study of a landscape your first choice is whether to put the horizon line high or low in the composition; avoid placing it in the middle as this tends to split the composition into halves.

I wanted this drawing to be principally about the drama of the dark blue sky with the white cliff in sharp relief against it, so I placed the horizon very low to make a strong sculptural composition. The figures are on the same plane as the viewer, making us very aware of the vertiginous nature of the cliff that rears above them.

Here my viewpoint is from high up on the cliffs and the horizon line has moved up with me. Three-quarters of the picture is of the cliffs and sea below and the figures are spread out in a diagonal composition. Although in narrative terms they are more static than the figures playing on the beach, they are compositionally more dynamic.

STILL LIFE

Still life subjects are the only chance the artist has to take complete control over composition, shape, colour and tone. You can choose your subject matter from everyday domestic details such as pots and pans or perhaps make a still life with a narrative theme such as wellington boots, a rod, a creel and some fish – evidence of a good day out. Choose objects that have something in common and use them to explore ways of showing form and surface.

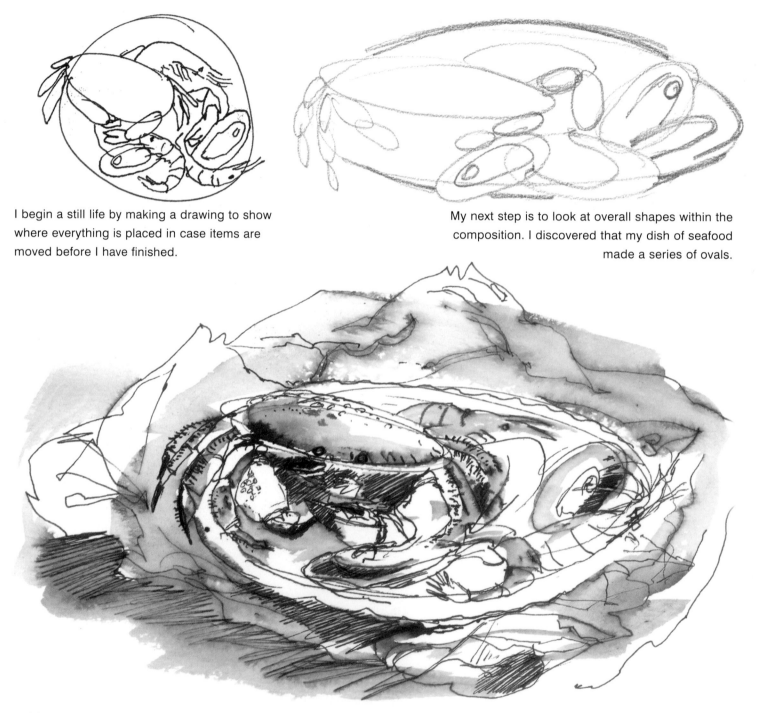

I begin a still life by making a drawing to show where everything is placed in case items are moved before I have finished.

My next step is to look at overall shapes within the composition. I discovered that my dish of seafood made a series of ovals.

Making a preliminary drawing with line and tone introduces you to some of the details of the drawing. In doing this pen and wash sketch I discovered I particularly liked the hairy legs of the crab and the softness of the supermarket carrier bag.

When you draw a still life, give yourself a time limit and see what results you can achieve over that period. I like the drawing below in all its stages, from its loose impressionist beginning to the final rich, illustrative state. If you lay masks over the page and look at each section in isolation you will be surprised by how different they are. How worked up you choose to make your own drawings is purely a matter of what suits your temperament.

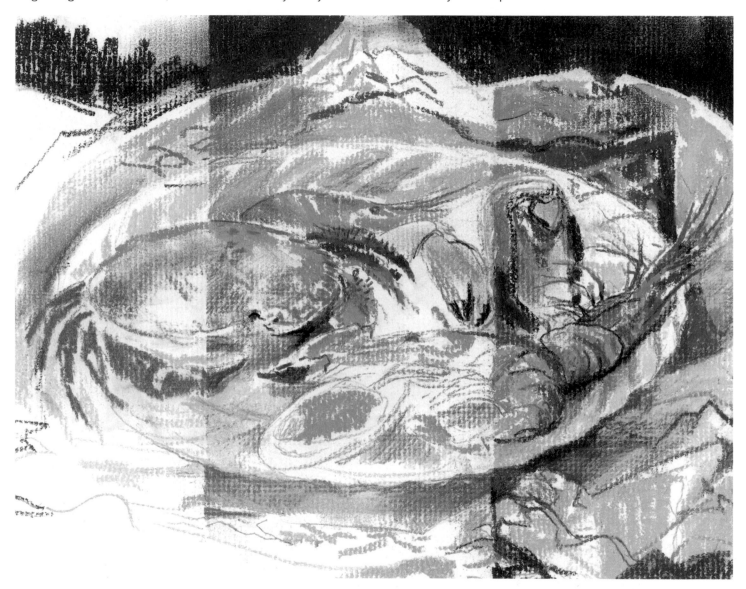

Once I was happy with the composition, I chose a lightly textured off-white paper to draw on. The illustration shows the three different stages of my working process. I laid in the whole drawing in the style seen in the left-hand side, establishing very loose linework and rubbing in broad areas of tone to identify the colours I would use. I then covered up the left-hand side of the paper and worked the drawing up further with more detailed tone and colour. The final stage shows what I felt to be the completed work.

FIGURES

Adding small figures to a picture will give some scale and narrative and it is not difficult to do; just a few lines and splashes of colour are sufficient to allow the viewer's imagination to put in the rest. Life drawing, however, is one of the most challenging areas for an artist and because mistakes show up so clearly it is the best learning experience you can have. Enrolling at a life drawing class at a local college will prove immensely rewarding.

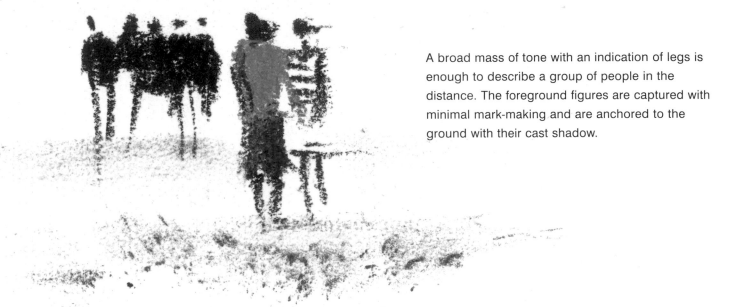

A broad mass of tone with an indication of legs is enough to describe a group of people in the distance. The foreground figures are captured with minimal mark-making and are anchored to the ground with their cast shadow.

In this drawing, light and dark areas are put in against a midtone. Here the colour is used mainly as tone to show the form of the model.

Most of the figure is lighter than the paper, while a lot of the browns are exactly the same tone. The figure is established here by the use of colour.

Nearly all the marks here are lighter than the background paper, including the subtle recessive shadows on the underside of the arm. The strength of colour and dispersal of tones in these three drawings by Gaynor Lloyd are in fact very similar, demonstrating how much pastel is affected by the surface it is used on. They show an artist studying the relationship of tones within the body without being deflected by the tone of the background.

When you are travelling, you will find it especially enjoyable to include figures in your pictures to capture the feel of the local life. Whether they are shopping at market, fishing, farming or enjoying leisure activities, the figures will bring atmosphere and vivacity to your drawings. If you feel self-conscious about people looking over your shoulder to see what you are doing, you can position yourself unobtrusively against a wall to work unnoticed.

This market stall scene in a little Tuscan town gave me the opportunity to have some fun with narrative and to use strong colours in a variety of cools and warms, lights and darks. It is done on untreated cardboard taken from a boarded envelope.

ARCHITECTURE

Architecture has already been created by design, so it has specific structures, angles and mass. It usually has hard edges and often bright colours and strong tones, but if you treat all the objects in front of you as the same weight there is a danger that they will cancel each other out. Instead, you need to give some thought to how you will treat foreground buildings to differentiate them from less important or more distant structures.

The building on the left is lightly defined and given soft edges in order to make the building in the centre with hard shutters and darker windows come forward. The two cyclists have the strongest colours, bringing them into the foreground. Note how the colours are echoed in the building above them.

The soft blue of the roof on the left-hand building is a recessive colour, and the windows are barely indicated. The viewer's eye understands them as windows that are too distant to see detail.

The two cyclists were quickly put in with just a few strokes of colour but they nevertheless play an important part in adding narrative and establishing foreground.

INTERIORS

When you enter a building, allow some time for your eyes to adjust to the dimmer light. This is particularly important on a bright sunny day, when it may take as long as ten minutes before you can fully interpret all the tones. The light sources inside a building can be quite complicated, so you need to take careful note of where shadows fall.

In this interior of the Opera House in Paris, light is flooding in from the doorway on the left, catching the figures as they walk in. There is another light source on the right, coming through the window straight ahead of us.

The left-hand side of the picture is mainly about colour as tone, with the little halo of light catching the figures from behind and making them stand out against blue shadows.

The cold, hard light from the window, done with simple white chalk, throws all the tone in front of it into high drama. There is hardly any colour in this side of the picture.

WATERCOLOUR PENCILS

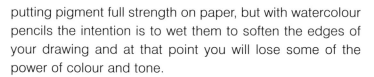

Watercolour pencils do not need fixing, so they are very convenient if you want to go out with minimal drawing equipment. However, you cannot obtain quite such strong colours from them. When you use dry pastels you are putting pigment full strength on paper, but with watercolour pencils the intention is to wet them to soften the edges of your drawing and at that point you will lose some of the power of colour and tone.

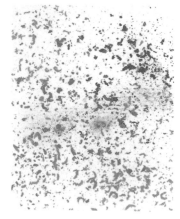

You can treat watercolour pencils like pastels and use them dry if you wish to, making colours by crosshatching two pigments. Alternatively, adding water will blend them together.

I scraped dust off the end of three pencils, then sprayed it with a fine mist of water to dissolve it.

After laying down clean water I worked pencils into it so that they dissolved at the tip, giving maximum colour.

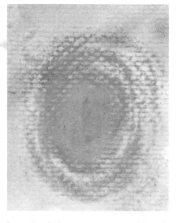

I wetted the paper, scrubbed in a little swatch of blue and then pushed it around with my finger to see how much of it would stay precise and how much would dissolve.

All the primary colours plus green stay crisp and bright while dry but are muddy when dissolved. Wetting two primary colours will give a pure secondary colour.

To the left of the red line, the flower is as it was drawn. I covered that side and sprayed the righthand side with a lot of water which took five minutes to dry, allowing the drawing to dissolve.

This drawing shows a little wild patch of my garden with the remains of some forget-me-nots in the foreground. Some of the drawing remains hard, while elsewhere I worked a loose wash of reds. As watercolour pencil is quite a transparent medium you cannot lay light colours over darker ones, so I reverted to a pastel technique of jabbing indentations in the paper, pulling the colour over it and leaving it dry. Wetting it would have caused it to flood into the indentations.

The forget-me-nots were created by indenting the paper with light marks, midtones and dark blues, giving the impression of numerous tiny flowers. I could then pull a darker tone over the flat of the paper.

WATERCOLOUR PASTELS

Where watercolour pencils are encased in wood in the same way as everyday graphic pencils, watercolour pastels come in chunky lengths like pieces of chalk. Consequently, you would not choose them for the precise work for which the pencils are ideal but for strong, fluid drawing you will find them very rewarding. Which you prefer will depend upon your temperament and also upon what you are trying to describe in your work.

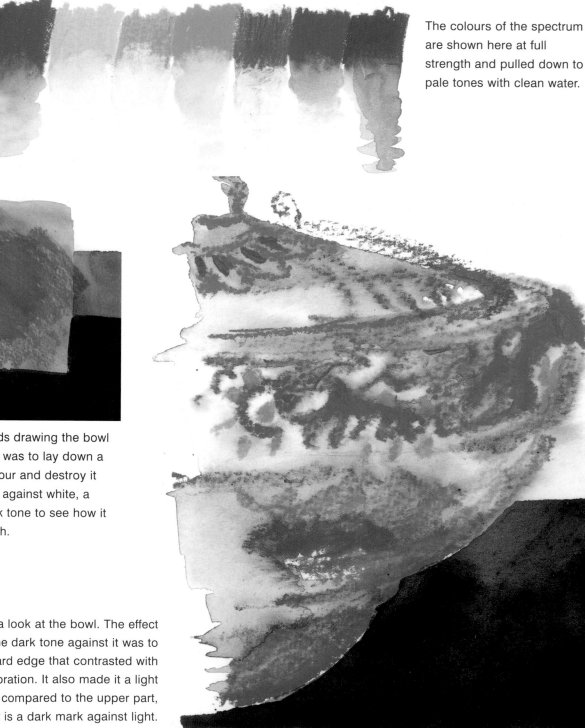

The colours of the spectrum are shown here at full strength and pulled down to pale tones with clean water.

My first step towards drawing the bowl on the facing page was to lay down a swatch of watercolour and destroy it with water. I tried it against white, a midtone and a dark tone to see how it looked against each.

Next I had a look at the bowl. The effect of putting the dark tone against it was to give it a hard edge that contrasted with its soft decoration. It also made it a light mark as compared to the upper part, where it is a dark mark against light.

I filled the bowl with potpourri, which has particularly interesting shapes and colours for an artist, then set to work. In some areas I wetted the paper before applying paint, while in others I drew on dry paper and destroyed the line with a wet brush.

OIL PASTELS

Unless they are using them to make an underdrawing for an oil painting on canvas, artists generally draw with oil pastels onto paper. However, it is necessary to prime the paper first to prevent the oil spreading out from the colour over a matter of time. A thin wash of acrylic primer, available from art shops, will suffice for this. Clean your brushes with distilled turpentine, and make sure you keep them separate from your watercolour brushes.

Oil pastels are brilliant in colour when used full strength and you can reduce them to lustrous transparent washes by thinning them with pure turpentine (not distilled turpentine, which may damage your paper).

Oil pastels act as a resist for watercolour. The first marks I made in this sketch were the colours of the women's clothes, which remained unchanged when I laid dark watercolour washes over the top of them.

The strong, vibrant colours of oil pastels are ideal for a decorative piece such as this. I drew the pastels directly on to the primed paper and then dissolved and spread them with a brush loaded with turpentine.

In this tonally dramatic picture painted *contre jour* (against the light), oil pastel has been used both as a resist for watercolour and on top of it.

The sparkly lights in the wet foreground were made by using oil pastel to lay light marks over dark ones, which is not possible with watercolour alone.

This detail shows the soft-edged marks I made with the oil pastel at the top of the painting. I then laid watercolour washes over the top.

CHARCOAL

Although charcoal is crumbly and dusty, it is capable of the most delicate work as well as tonally powerful drawings. It is undeniably messy and doesn't appeal to everyone, but do try it out. Even if you decide you don't like it, you will have learnt more about mark-making just by using it. You will find this particularly valuable if you are prone to drawing very tightly, for it will encourage you to make bold gestural marks which you can then translate to another medium.

In this life drawing Gaynor Lloyd has described the form of the model by the changing weight of the line, which varies from thick to thin. The sparse, soft lines up the back develop into the more fully described head with its shadowed, half-hidden features.

CHARCOAL WITH WATERCOLOUR

Perhaps surprisingly, charcoal works very well with watercolour washes, which tend to be associated with delicacy and translucency. The charcoal gives a tough drawing and when you begin laying the washes over it they pick up a lot of granular quality that produces lovely textured areas of paint.

Watercolour over charcoal gave me gritty washes that were just right for the gritty subject matter of an old steam train boiler.

Sitting in a car park on a wet and windy day, I made quick charcoal notes about the people queuing at the ticket machine and washed some paint over the top. This sketch sums up the briskness of the scene and gives a feel of the weather conditions.

A MIXED MEDIA PIECE

In these drawings of Venice I enjoyed pushing pastels to their extremes, using them together with watercolour pencils and charcoal. While the subject matter was a visual delight, the pleasure of painting and drawing is partly about experiencing the handling of materials and the richness of design, colour and texture for their own sake. As an artist, you can become intrigued by these challenges even when you are tackling the most mundane objects.

As preparation for a drawing of the Basilica in Venice I made an initial drawing on wet white paper in my sketchbook. My aim was to explore all the aspects of the light falling on the Basilica and the shadows thrown by the bell tower on the wet foreground, as well as the balance of the hard delineation of the scaffolding against the crumbly façade of the Basilica.

Back in the studio, I explored how I might use colour and texture, hard and soft lines and extremes of tone to regenerate the excitement I felt when I was on location.

Next I began to examine the two-point perspective in the foreground and how I could make that surface echo the buildings behind. I solved this by drawing the top of the buildings shown here with quite hard pastel pencil and then using clean water on a soft brush to pull some of those tones down into the foreground. I exaggerated the perspective a little to add excitement.

The Basilica, Venice 28 × 38 cm (11 × 15 in)

This final piece shows the accumulation of all decisions made as a result of making the preliminary studies. I have introduced the red banners that hang from the flagpoles in front of the Basilica and the figures are now established as little points of colour, some light on dark and others dark on light. They are harder-edged in the foreground and softer-edged and more muted in colour as they recede in the picture plane, contributing to the three-dimensional effect given by the single-point perspective.

A MIXED MEDIA PIECE

This detail shows the brilliant colour of which pastel is capable and the vigorously textured effects you can obtain in linear and tonal work. The latter make it especially suited to describing the mass and surface of architecture such as the Basilica.